MORISOT

Berthe Morisot

by JEAN DOMINIQUE REY

BONFINI PRESS

Title page: SELF-PORTRAIT, 1885
Oil on canvas, 28¼″ × 35¾″ (72 × 91 cm)
Private collection

Translated from the French by:
SHIRLEY JENNINGS

Collection published under the direction of:
MADELEINE LEDIVELEC-GLOECKNER

PHOTOGRAPHS

Bulloz, Paris – A. E. Dolinski, San Gabriel, California – J. Hyde, Paris – Claude Mercier, Geneva – Eric Pollitzer, New York – Tom Scott, Edinburgh – Service de Documentation Photographique de la Réunion des Musées Nationaux, Paris – Studio Lourmel 77, Paris – Ole Woldbye, Copenhagen.

PRINTED IN ITALY BY INDUSTRIE GRAFICHE CATTANEO, S.P.A. - BERGAMO
© 1982 BY BONFINI PRESS, INC., NAEFELS, SWITZERLAND

1394

PORTRAIT OF MADAME HUBARD, 1874. Oil on canvas, 19⅞″ 31⅞″ (50.5 × 81 cm)
Ordrupgaardsamlingen, Copenhagen

Berthe Morisot's work shows no sign of aging. Apart from the period costumes, the pictures might have been painted yesterday.

Perhaps the most obvious explanation is that they have been less popularized and reproduced than other Impressionist paintings and so have not become overly familiar. Yet if we find their charm still unspoiled today, this is due to other qualities than a mere accident of history, not least the happy mixture of freshness and subtlety that is characteristic of Morisot's smooth, finely poised style.

The pictures are as discreet as the artist who painted them. There is no excessive display in this understated art that only reveals its true value with the passing of the years. Morisot's work goes far deeper than the impression it gives of capturing only the transient fruit, the fleeting moment, the pollen that will soon blow away. Here the first impression is no more than a mask imposed by the artist's reticence: If everything appears suggestive,

THATCHED COTTAGE IN NORMANDY, 1865
Oil on canvas, 18″ × 21⅝″ (46 × 55 cm)
Private Collection

THE ARTIST'S SISTER AT A WINDOW, 1869
Oil on canvas, 21¼″ × 17¾″ (54 × 45 cm)
National Gallery of Art, Washington, D.C. ▷
Ailsa Mellon Bruce Collection

6

allusive, never for an instant labored, reality has nevertheless been grasped, however unobtrusively, in a style that is both delicate and stripped to essentials. Hence the fact that after all this time the pictures still look new and modern — as if the paint had scarcely had time to dry. Now that the work of Berthe Morisot has become part of history, we can appreciate the artist's true worth, finding that she bears comparison with the greatest names of the past.

Before discussing Morisot's art, let us look for a moment at the beautiful face portrayed by Manet and which the artist herself several times tried to paint. Perhaps in the most classical of her self-portraits she made herself look deliberately severe, but at the same time we cannot fail to be struck by the intriguing blend of charm and intelligence, sensuousness and anxiety, modesty and decisiveness, enthusiasm and misgivings. In fact, the impression is even stronger in another, more boldly drawn *Self-Portrait*,* painted on an unprepared canvas. And it was the conflict and reconciliation of these qualities that would be transposed and find fulfillment in her work, while at the same time being reflected in her letters, her friendships, and her life.

If we wish to understand her work, we must never forget that Morisot's gentle manner concealed an iron will that nothing would deflect from her chosen path. Her art required immense determination yet never once revealed the effort or tenacity involved. Like all great art it effaces every hint of the growth process to leave nothing but the finished flower.

*

*　　　*

Berthe Morisot was born on January 15, 1841, the same year as Frédéric Bazille and Auguste Renoir. Her birthplace was Bourges in the exact center of France, but her family was typically Parisian. Her father, Edmé-Tiburce Morisot, was a prefect but had been destined to become an architect like his father of the same name. Jean-Honoré Fragonard was a distant relation of her grandparents' generation, and his son, Evariste Fragonard, painted a portrait of Madame Morisot, the architect's wife.

More important than the blood relationship, however, is the fact that Berthe Morisot and the great Fragonard shared not only a preference for feminine subjects but also a certain similarity of style, with their light, decisive, rapid touch, as if the brush no more than skimmed the surface of the canvas, scattering colors like roses on a dress.

*

*　　　*

All the good fairies seem to have been present at Berthe Morisot's christening, and perhaps the most surprising thing about her career as a painter is that, having been showered with every kind of gift, she never succumbed to facility but became a great artist with all the struggles and perseverance which that involves.

---

* See title page.

THE HARBOR AT LORIENT, 1869. Oil on canvas, $16^{15}/_{16}''$ × $28^3/_8''$ (43 × 72 cm)
National Gallery of Art, Washington, D.C. Ailsa Mellon Bruce Collection

She appears to have led a peaceful life. And biographers avid for anecdotes find little to satisfy them in this tranquil existence where events seem to glide past as gracefully as a swan on a lake.

Morisot's good fortune and untroubled life are to be explained by both the age in which she lived and her social background. But here too a miracle occurred. No one in this family of the *haute bourgeoisie* opposed her vocation, and, in fact, it was deliberately encouraged. Berthe was lucky indeed to be painting under the Second Empire at a time when history seemed to fall silent for a moment before once more striking up its customary stridencies. Did her parents have any premonition that she would become a great artist? Or did they merely allow her to do as she wished? There is no doubt that Berthe had her mother's support. She herself was never satisfied with her painting but constantly striving for perfection.

*
*   *

In setting the scene for Berthe Morisot's work, it is interesting to note that during all her adult life she lived in a single area of Paris. She never returned to Bourges and her early years were spent in a number of towns where her father was appointed prefect. But in 1855 the family moved to Rue des Moulins (now Rue Scheffer) in Paris, and afterward to the neighboring Rue Franklin. Berthe subsequently lived in Rue Guichard and Avenue d'Eylau, spending most of her life in Rue de Villejust, which she left for Rue Weber shortly before her death in 1895. She is buried in the Passy cemetery, close to the Rue des Moulins where her Parisian existence began. Few lives have been passed in such a narrow circle, in the heart of a single district.

Berthe Morisot never had very far to go to find the transient or permanent subjects that emerged so fresh from her canvas. Rue Franklin was in a country district and her parents' house was surrounded by a garden in which she had her first studio. And the home in Rue de Villejust looked out over fields in a peaceful area near the Bois de Boulogne where she could paint the ladies strolling by, the lake, the trees, and the swans.

It is true that Berthe Morisot traveled more than many of her contemporaries, in turn visiting Spain, England, the Channel Isles, Italy, Belgium, and Holland, while she often made trips in France itself. But every one of these journeys or visits, during which she would paint or look at museums, provided no more than an inspiration for her art which was always perfected at home in her studio.

In fact, the word studio is almost an exaggeration. For a great many years Berthe Morisot painted in the rooms in which she lived, making no distinction between work and everyday life. At the same time, as soon as a visitor was announced, canvas, brushes, and paints were hidden in a cupboard or, in Rue de Villejust, behind a screen. The practice indicates not only the painter's modesty, but also the fact that her art was always closely bound up with her life.

*
*   *

Bibi at Vassé, 1889. Pencil, 7³⁄₄″ × 10¹⁄₄″ (19.5 × 26 cm)
Private Collection, Paris

THE ARTIST'S SISTER, MADAME PONTILLON, SEATED ON THE GRASS, 1867
Oil on canvas, 17³/₄" × 28¹/₂" (46 × 72 cm)
The Cleveland Museum of Art

We know very little about Berthe Morisot's childhood, except that she liked reading, enjoyed Shakespeare at an early age, and was fond of modeling simple objects out of mud and clay.

Berthe had piano lessons with a famous musician named Stamaty. In the music room hung a magnificent drawing of the pianist and his family by J.D. Ingres. The picture was perhaps the young Berthe's first contact with living art, and we can imagine her eyes straying in the middle of her lessons from the model to the drawing and back again.

This was not, however, the origin of her vocation. Berthe's decision to become an artist was triggered by a trivial incident, one of those unimportant everyday events that have enormous and unexpected consequences. In 1857 when Berthe was sixteen, her mother wanted to give her father a surprise by getting his three daughters to make drawings for him. The girls were taken to have lessons from Chocarne in Rue de Lille. But the apprenticeship was of short duration. Yves, the eldest, soon gave up drawing, while Edma and Berthe developed a taste for it, and it was not long before they were demanding a less conventional teacher. The two sisters continued to work together for twelve years until Edma gave up painting when she married. Only Berthe persevered and devoted her life to art.

Apart from Chocarne, all her teachers had some inkling of Berthe Morisot's gifts. Certainly this was true of Guichard, who lived near them in Passy, and who taught the two sisters the rudiments of painting. The very first lesson consisted in painting a picture exclusively in white in order to learn the values of light and shade. Later he took them to study the Venetian paintings in the Louvre. It was not long, however, before he realized he had nothing more to teach them, and because Berthe was insisting on painting outside, a heresy in the eyes of the historical painter, Guichard decided to introduce the sisters to Corot. Berthe's independence may well have surprised Corot who got them to copy a number of his works — Berthe's copy of the *View of Tivoli* is still in existence — and afterward sent the two sisters to study with Oudinot who lived at Auvers-sur-Oise, where they soon got to know Daubigny, Daumier, and Guillemet.

In 1863 the two young women set up house at Chou, a small hamlet between Pontoise and Auvers, which we can imagine today by looking at the etching by Paul Gachet. It was no more than a few peasant houses clinging to the cliff above a towpath, a scene that was soon to be painted by Pissarro, Cézanne, and afterward Loiseau. Today, only one picture painted there by Berthe Morisot survives — *Old Lane at Auvers*, which is reminiscent of Corot but differs from him in the freedom of style that a number of contemporary painters were beginning to develop. It is the first work that Morisot exhibited at the Salon, in 1864.

The same year the Morisots rented Léon Riesener's country house at Beuzeval in Normandy. It was the beginning of a new series of friendships. Léon Riesener, grandson of the famous cabinetmaker and a cousin of Delacroix, was himself a painter who actively encouraged Berthe Morisot's innovations. Riesener's daughter Rosalie was to become one of Morisot's favorite models. In Riesener's house in Cours-la-Reine Berthe met the sculptor Marcello, alias the beautiful Duchess Castiglione Colonna, who painted her portrait in oils in 1875. Morisot became interested in sculpture, which she studied with Aimé Millet, in later years making a bust of her daughter Julie.

It is time to examine what remains of Berthe Morisot's early work — she destroyed a considerable number of her first attempts — once she had got beyond the stage of copying the old masters in the Louvre (Veronese) or assimilating Corot's early lessons.

Julie with a Mandoline, 1889. Lead pencil, 7½" × 5⅞" (19 × 15 cm)
Private Collection, Paris

*Thatched Cottage in Normandy** is a pure landscape, which is unusual in Berthe Morisot's work, and already shows her characteristic charm and precision, as if reality and mystery were inextricably mingled.   Clearly there are echoes of Corot, but the picture looks forward to the Impressionist use of light.   The grass appears soft and fluffy, scattered with little flecks that catch the diffused light, which is thrown back by the graceful trunks of the birches.

It is not possible to discuss in detail here all the works through which Berthe Morisot learned her art.   What is striking, however, in the pictures painted at Auvers, in Normandy, and afterward at Pont-Aven—famous places in the history of painting where Berthe was sometimes the first to tread—is not so much the still perceptible influence of her masters as her very personal sense of light.

Let us go on to the first pictures in which she found her own individual style, for example, *The Artist's Sister, Madame Pontillon, Seated on the Grass,*** painted in 1867 at Petites Dalles near Fécamp, where twelve years later Monet painted his views of the cliffs. On the grass, in a landscape which is no more than a background, a young woman is reading with her fan lying on the ground beside her.   The three touches of black—on her bosom, at her throat, and on her hat—contrast with the bright colors of the rest of the picture and make them sing.

If we had to define Berthe Morisot's originality—the quality that really distinguishes her from her contemporaries—we might describe her as a painter of the early morning light. And for that Corot is responsible.   Better than any other painter, she captured—but that is almost too strong—conveyed on her canvases the pale gold of the dawn.

The year 1868 marks a turning point in her life.   One morning in the Louvre Museum where she was copying a Rubens with her friend Rosalie Riesener, Berthe Morisot met Edouard Manet.   Fantin-Latour introduced them.   It was a strange meeting of painters, uniting past and future.

However much he was opposed, discussed, criticized, and ignored, Manet was still a distinguished older painter to the young generation.   From the time of their first meeting, there sprung up a lasting friendship; indeed, it was a meeting of kindred spirits.   And yet the relationship has often been distorted or misunderstood, usually to the detriment of Berthe Morisot.

Naturally the aspiring artist was attracted by the personality of the famous older man and admired his work.   Manet, in turn, was dazzled by the young woman, for he was able to see not only her own promise but how much she could inspire in others.   He soon asked Berthe to pose for *The Balcony*, where she appears beside the landscape painter Guillemet whom she had met at Auvers-sur-Oise.   It was the first of eleven marvelous portraits that Manet made of her—paintings, drawings, and engravings—some of them bare but revealing sketches, others finished portraits in which he captured the very essence of her remarkable personality.   The most famous of them all was the portrait that Valéry rightly considered to be among Manet's greatest works.   It was painted in a few hours, before dinner.   The year was 1874, when Berthe Morisot was making up her mind to marry the painter's brother. The eyes beneath the black ringlets burn like dark coals—the sharp eyes of the painter but also the eyes of the woman in whom melancholy mingles with passion.   It is a portrait that

---

* See page 6.   ** See page 12.

goes beyond appearances and one that we never tire of looking at. It seems to contain all that the two painters shared: their friendship, their exchange of ideas, and their mutual inspiration. And the somewhat distant air of independence, that look of remoteness tinged with sadness, is a telling definition of Berthe Morisot's character.

Here it is time to dispose of the mistaken opinion that Morisot was a pupil of Manet. It is true that Manet initially gave her a certain amount of advice and encouragement, once even touching up one of her pictures (*The Mother and Sister of the Artist*, 1869–1870, National Gallery, Washington, D.C.), but he never regarded her as either a student or a follower. This, however, is the version that has been repeated since the first article on the subject by Zola, in 1880: «Madame Berthe Morizot [sic] is a very personal pupil of Edouard Manet» («Le Naturalisme au Salon»), or the statement by Huysmans the following year: «like M. Manet, her master, Mme. Morizot [sic] undoubtedly possesses an eye...» («L'Exposition des Indépendants en 1881»). Since then the refrain has been echoed through our own day in hastily written reviews or entries in dictionaries, monotonously handing down the same clichés and the same mistakes.

The modern age has become so censorious of influences that it either sees them as one-sided, or denies them altogether.

It is true that Berthe Morisot, like the majority of the Impressionists, was at first influenced by Manet, and that like them, she occasionally painted the same subjects as the older artist. Yet, as we shall see, it is easy to show that Manet, who was always on the lookout for new themes, sometimes borrowed ideas from Morisot. In any case, Berthe Morisot's subjects were always treated in an entirely personal style, like her *Picnic*, which is more intimate than Manet's, being reduced to a single couple, perhaps the only one she ever painted (1875). She not only inspired Manet as a portraitist, but as a painter she formed a link between him and the Impressionists that enabled him to understand ideas he had originally rejected. It is, in fact, quite legitimate to speak of Berthe Morisot's influence on Manet during his last years, as if in the end their roles were reversed.

*
*   *

Let us return to Berthe Morisot's own work during these decisive years. At first, and indeed throughout her life, Morisot painted those closest to her — at this period her mother and her sister. After sharing painting lessons with Berthe, Edma became her sister's favorite model. She is the subject of *The Mother and Sister of the Artist* (1869–1870) and of *The Artist's Sister at a Window*, where she is seen opening a fan with a dreamy air. And soon she would appear in the famous *Cradle* (1872, Louvre Museum), Berthe Morisot's best-known picture, where Edma is the young mother watching her baby asleep beneath the draperies of the cradle, the whole picture illumined by the contrast between the delicate white curtains and the black of the mother's hair and dress. But the most striking picture of Morisot's family at the time is the *Interior** painted in Rue Franklin in 1872. The group on the left foreshadows the picture *On the Balcony* that she would paint two years later of the same balcony, here just glimpsed through the half-open window. In this first

---

* See front cover.

16

PORTRAIT OF MADAME PONTILLON, 1871. Pastel, 31⅞″ × 25⅝″ (81 × 65 cm)
Musée du Louvre, Cabinet des Dessins, Paris

The Artist's Sister Edma with
her Daughter Jeanne, 1872
Watercolor, 8⅝″ × 8¼″ (22 × 21 cm)
National Gallery of Art, Washington, D.C.
Ailsa Mellon Bruce Collection

On the Sofa, 1871
Watercolor, 7¹/₁₆″ × 5¹/₂″ (18 × 14 cm) ▷
Nationalmuseum, Stockholm

On the Balcony, before 1874. Watercolor over graphite, 8⅛″ × 6⅞″ (20.6 × 17.5 cm)
The Art Institute of Chicago. Gift in memory of Charles Netcher II

picture, however, the woman and child are pale figures (the woman has a light gray dress and fair hair), and the gap in the curtains seems to be a symbol of expectation. By contrast, the young woman seen in profile in the center is dressed all in black and appears unutterably calm, while behind her, to the right, the green and red of a profusion of plants emerges from a jardinière. Berthe Morisot painted the same plants in the background of her picture *At the Ball*,* but with broader brushstrokes and with the addition of some touches of yellow to echo the flowers in the young girl's hair and dress. It is often possible to follow certain details from one picture to another, although they are not so much repeated as used for new purposes in a different combination. It is as if the scenery were shifted slowly under the painter's watchful eye, depending on the needs of the representation.

There is another aspect of Berthe Morisot's work that we find fascinating today and that has not perhaps received sufficient attention. She began by painting the city, a changing Paris that now seems hard to imagine (*The Seine at the Pont d'Iéna*, 1866, *View of Paris from the Trocadéro*, 1872, *Landscape at Genevilliers*, 1875). At the same time she emerges, in these and similar pictures, as a painter of «fleeting modernity.» Perhaps she had heard this favorite expression of Baudelaire when she was with the Manets. In all probability, the idea was in the air and the new subjects were providing painters with opportunities for experiments that would lead to their rediscovery of light.

On the Balcony is the most beautiful of these urban views: a young woman in black (Edma Pontillon) leans on the rail with a red-haired child (Paule Gobillard) in a white dress beside her, looking out over a garden that we cannot see. There is still a trace of Manet in the black dress, but the composition is original and typical of Morisot: the vast horizon of the city with the blue river glimpsed between the balcony and the empty Champ de Mars, gives to the woman and child a strange dimension of mingled absence and presence, evoking the clarity of a dream. A watercolor** gives us a first idea of the picture. It is composed of dark and light areas of paint and the style is allusives whereas on the canvas, the landscape is pushed into the background and the picture becomes a symphony of answering colors: the brown of the wall, the red of the flowers, the black of the dress, and the gold of the dome are all picked up in other details of the painting. The picture is one of Berthe Morisot's key works, representing both a beginning and an end, a synthesis and a new departure.

Gradually, however, she became more interested in nature than in the city, and in this she was faithful to the newly emerging Impressionism. At the same time she did not relinquish her preoccupation with modernism as we shall see in discussing some of her most lovely female figures.

The fact that right from the outset the Impressionist group included a woman appears symbolic today, and shows that the revolution in art was not confined to painting but presaged other, more far-reaching changes in society.

*

*   *

Throughout her life, whenever she painted a picture or took part in an exhibition, Berthe Morisot was considered an equal by the other Impressionist painters, all of whom held her work in high esteem. Manet, the distinguished elder painter who only joined the

---

* See page 36.   ** See page 20.

HIDE-AND-SEEK, 1873. Oil on canvas, 17¾″ × 21⅝″ (45 × 55 cm)
Private Collection

CATCHING BUTTERFLIES, 1874. Oil on canvas, 18″ × 22¹/₁₆″ (46 × 56 cm)
Musée du Jeu de Paume, Paris

group at the insistence of Berthe Morisot; Degas, who remained on the fringes of Impressionism, at once cautious and inventive; Renoir and Monet who were the leading spirits and the most typical painters of the movement: all of them admired Morisot's craftsmanship and spontaneous style, and wanted to own her pictures. At a very early stage, Manet acquired *The Harbor at Lorient,** a poem in blue and brown, where all the light from the sky and the sea is reflected in the white dress of the young woman seated on the jetty wall as if she were the living signature of the artist. Pissarro owned the *View of Tivoli*, which is marked by the influence of Corot by whom it was inspired. And somewhat later Degas acquired a picture painted at Fécamp in 1874: *In a Villa at the Seaside.*** In fact, this picture exists in two versions with the woman alternately on the right and on the left. And here we can already see the unobtrusive treatment of the human figure which, with the rise of Impressionism, would become an integral part of the landscape. Strangely enough, two inseparable friends, Edgar Degas and Henri Rouart, were each determined to get hold of one of the pair of pictures. The version chosen by Degas is slightly more mysterious, conveying an atmosphere of expectation and suspense, almost but not quite belied by the smooth eau-de-Nil of the sea, the dark blue of the skirt trimmed with white edged flounces like so many little waves, and the delicate pink of the sky. No wonder Degas admired the bold way the wooden balcony is cut out, so that ships can be seen sailing between the posts. Incidentally, yet another proof that Degas was far from being a dyed-in-the-wool misogynist is that he was among the first to champion the work of three remarkably gifted women: Berthe Morisot, Mary Cassatt, and Suzanne Valadon.

The Impressionists, who have been seen as nature lovers in harmony with the developing industrial society, are more accurately described as artists who captured with rare felicity, and in an entirely original style, a world on the point of vanishing precisely because of the growth of industry. They recorded with the lightest touches a natural environment that was to be steadily eroded and the fleeting scenes that industrial development would soon erase. Paradoxically, the fleeting moments have achieved permanence at the hands of the Impressionists, and even today their spontaneous description of a disappearing countryside, their miraculous reconciliation of vision and reality, seem closer to us than all that has sought to replace them. Hence, the amazing fascination that Impressionism continues to exert a century later.

Although everyone remembers Pissarro's meadows, Monet's poppy fields, and Renoir's grassy paths, the landscapes of Berthe Morisot deserve as much attention. The watercolor entitled *Young Woman and Child Sitting in the Grass**** is one of the most suggestive of her landscapes, while still retaining her lightness of touch and bold style. In the distance the faint blue of a town and its windmills are outlined against a pale sky. But here the woman and child would seem more important than the landscape were it not that they are so much a part of the field and the sky, two white patches on grass made golden by the sunlight. What the Impressionists were celebrating, with an extreme economy of means, was the harmony between man and nature, which the age was just beginning to rediscover in all its original simplicity, free from the trappings of myth and legend.

Although so much has already been written about the Impressionist movement, it is worth mentioning that there is something feminine about the very concept of Impressionism — the love of the transient moment and the fact that impressions are accorded more importance

---

* See page 9.   ** See page 25.   *** See page 49.

IN A VILLA AT THE SEASIDE, 1874. Oil on canvas, 19¾″ × 24⅛″ (51 × 61 cm)
Norton Simon, Inc. Museum of Art, Los Angeles

THE LILACS AT MAURECOURT, 1874. Oil on canvas, 19^{11}/$_{16}$″ × 24″ (51 × 61 cm)
Private Collection

ON THE LAWN, 1874. Pastel, 28¾″ × 36¼″ (73 × 92 cm)
Musée du Petit Palais, Paris

WOMAN AND CHILD BY THE SEA, 1874. Watercolor, 4¾″ × 6¾″ (12 × 16 cm)
Private Collection

than perception. It is therefore not surprising that it was possibly the first movement in the history of painting to include a woman among its founder members, and in fact Morisot remained the group's most stable element over the years. Later she was joined by another woman, Mary Cassatt, who played a part in making Impressionism a success in America. Nevertheless, Berthe Morisot remains the painter who expressed with the greatest skill and delicacy the emphasis on the fugitive and the preeminence of sensation over reminiscence that were to open up new avenues for artists and transform the whole art of painting.

It is true that the critics were not as hard on her as they were on Manet and then Monet, and afterward Cézanne. With the honorable exception of Burty, this did not, however, prevent them from misspelling her name — even Zola and Huysmans writing it with a «z» instead of an «s.» The trend was common enough at the time: Cisley, Degaz, and Sésame — slips of this kind may well be partly due to haste but sometimes are clearly indicative of the contempt in which new artists are held.

Like the others, Berthe Morisot did not escape the ironic comments of Louis Leroy in «Charivari» in 1874: «Don't talk to me about Mlle Morisot! That young lady does not waste time on reproducing a host of boring details. When she has a hand to paint, she simply applies as many brushstrokes as there are fingers and the job is done!» It was not long, however, before the critics began to describe her talent in more appropriate terms. For example, Georges Rivière, who referred to «the unexpected and feminine charm of Mademoiselle Morisot» in 1877, was soon writing as follows:

> Her watercolors, pastels and paintings all have ... the light unpretentious style that makes us admire her. Mademoiselle Morisot has an eye of extraordinary sensibility. ... How pretty is the picture of the young woman in a pink housecoat lying on a sofa. And how enchanting is the woman at her toilette, or the woman in front of the looking glass. Above there hangs a charming little landscape full of greenery and sunshine with a woman in a blue dress. Madame Berthe Morisot has captured on her canvas the most fugitive notes, with a delicacy, a skill and a technique which earn her a place in the forefront of the Impressionist group.

The pictures referred to by Rivière are in fact among the most successfull ones she painted at that time. The woman in the blue dress in the somewhat sad figure of *In a Villa at the Seaside.* The young woman in the housecoat is undoubtedly the superb *Portrait of Madame Hubard,* * now in Denmark, and which is one of the major works not only of Berthe Morisot but of the entire period. On a bed with a white pillow and a slightly bluish valance, a woman dressed all in white and pink organdy and tulle lies gazing at us with eyes as black as her hair. The wall in the background is barely indicated. The woman is holding an open fan; its yellow folds echo the color of her slippers, while the base of the fan is black, picked out in red and blue. The picture possesses a mixture of charm and sensuality that only a woman could achieve, for it requires a power of identification and a knowledge of the female character that too often eludes the male artist. Here already we can see a clear contrast with Manet. The undeniable modernism of the theme does not exclude total

---

* See page 5.

LITTLE BOY IN GREY, 1880. Oil on canvas, $33^7/_8'' \times 24^9/_{16}''$ (86 × 62 cm)
Private Collection

PAULE GOBILLARD, 1886. Pastel, 28¾″ × 22¾″ (73 × 60 cm)
Private Collection

Young Girl Seated at the Table, 1889
Pencil
The Art Institute of Chicago
Gift of Mr. and Mrs. Raymond J. Horowitz

YOUNG WOMAN POWDERING
HER FACE, 1877
Oil on canvas, 18″ × 15¹⁵/₁₆″ (46 × 38 cm) ▷
Musée du Jeu de Paume, Paris

Before the Mirror, 1890
Pencil, 11¾″ × 7⅞″ (30 × 20 cm)
▷ *Musée du Louvre,*
Cabinet des Dessins, Paris

LADY AT HER TOILETTE, c. 1880
Oil on canvas, 22¾″ × 31¾″ (60 × 80 cm)
The Art Institute of Chicago
Stickney Fund

AT THE BALL, 1875. Oil on canvas, 24³⁄₈″ × 20¹⁄₂″ (62 × 52 cm)
Musée Marmottan, Paris

assimilation with the model, which in both painting and literature was something very new at time. (We have only to remember Flaubert's cry: «Madame Bovary, c'est moi!») It is the emphasis on subjectivity that was to be one of the additional aspects of Impressionism and that perhaps only a woman could have carried so far.

The *Young Woman at her Toilette* mentioned by Rivière is probably the version later acquired by Mary Cassat. Between 1875 and 1877 Berthe Morisot painted a series of masterly variations on this theme. The *Woman at the Mirror* (private collection, Paris), whose real title might be *Asking Questions of the Mirror*, is a superb poem in white as if in homage to Guichard's first lesson. It has never been described more felicitously than by the artist's own daughter, Julie Manet, in her recently published «Diary,» when in 1899 she saw the picture again at the sale of Choquet's collection:

> A little woman in white, dressed in a light bonnet and looking at herself in a small hand mirror; she is sitting on an equally white sofa and is outlined against a curtain of white muslin through which streams the light which plays so delightfully over this whole symphony in white, while the shadows make the most astonishing shades of gray. What difficulties have been overcome with how much charm (page 236).

The white motif recurs in the *Young Woman Powdering her Face** painted in the same year 1877, and now in the Louvre. This picture, however, contains more color: areas of red like the lacquer box on the table, the corner of a cushion or the bottom of the armchair; hints of red in the pictures hanging on the yellow wall; and three minute touches of pink, a flower bud on the left, the young woman's lips and a flower pinned to the skirt of her dress, that make the whole picture sing in a subtle play of light and color. In spite of its small size, this work by Berthe Morisot bridges the gap between Modernism and the eighteenth century, combining the decorative style of Fragonard with the new discovery of the appeal of light colors.

The *Psyche* painted the preceding year shows a beautifully composed harmony of white (dress, curtains) and red (carpet), while the two colors merge in the Venetian red of the hair.

In these pictures we take for granted — not surprisingly a hundred years later — the great discovery of Impressionism: That light is not a beam falling on individual objects but a suffused radiance that comes from everywhere at once, intangible but always present.

*
*   *

We must now discuss that same light as it appears in the lovely pictures painted out of doors.

Shortly before the advent of Impressionism, at a time when the movement was already being foreshadowed by a number of artists, the Goncourt brothers, who almost alone at that date were more interested in the eighteenth century than in their own day, wrote in their

---

* See page 33.

EUGENE MANET AND HIS DAUGHTER AT BOUGIVAL, 1881. Oil on canvas, 28¾″ × 36¼″ (73 × 92 cm)
Private Collection

THE FABLE, 1883. Oil on canvas, 25⅝″ × 31⅞″ (65 × 81 cm)
Private Collection

Study for « Girl in a Green Coat »
undated
Pencil on paper, 6⅞″ × 4⅛″
(17.5 × 10.2 cm)
◁ *The Metropolitan Museum of Art*
New York
Robert Lehman Collection

SUMMER'S DAY, 1879
Oil on canvas, 18″ × 29½″
(46 × 75 cm)
National Gallery, London

ON THE VERANDA, 1884. Oil on canvas, 31⅞″ × 39⅜″ (81 × 100 cm)
Private Collection

EUGENE MANET AND HIS DAUGHTER IN THE GARDEN, 1883
Oil on canvas, 23⅝″ × 28¾″ (60 × 73 cm). Private Collection

YOUNG WOMAN RETYING HER SKATE, 1880
Oil on canvas, 18¹/₈″ × 21¹¹/₁₆″ (46 × 55 cm)
Private Collection

Bather, 1891
Pencil, 14⁵/₈″ × 17³/₄″ (37 × 45 cm) ▷
Private Collection

«Diary»: «Undoubtedly the cycle of great painting is closed . . . and only landscape remains» (December 1866). If they had but looked a little further they would have found great painting being done by Manet, or in a picture like Morisot's *Woman at the Mirror*, which ought to have enchanted them, except that these unrepentant misogynists never once mentioned the name of Berthe Morisot. They were, however, right about the importance of landscape painting.

The first time Berthe stayed with her sister Edma at Maurecourt, close to Chou and Auvers where she had painted her first landscapes, was in 1873, before the death of her father (January 1874) and her marriage to Eugène Manet (December 1874). Before that she had visited Spain (1872) and Petites Dalles (1873). She returned to Maurecourt in 1874, the date of the first Impressionist exhibition in which she took part. It was a key year in her development as an artist. She had shaken off the influence of Manet and the past and was now at the height of her powers. She began to paint some of her major works and indeed some of the most important Impressionist paintings, though a great many art historians, too shortsighted to appreciate a woman, often omit to mention or reproduce them.

One of her most successful outdoor paintings is *Hide-and-Seek* * where a young woman with a green parasol appears to be dancing around a bush covered in red flowers, while on the left a little girl wears a diminutive dress and heavy hat that seem to reflect and concentrate all the light in the sky. The landscape, with its glimpse of the river Oise, is painted in broad horizontal strokes against which the grass and bushes stand out in sharp contrast. One impression that recurs in a number of paintings by Morisot is that the landscape seems to be flowing from left to right like a mighty river or the ebbing away of life, while here the spiral movement of the two figures attempts to halt for a moment the passing of time.

The Lilacs at Maurecourt ** is another picture in which time is captured, concentrated, and seems almost motionless. It is a pattern of light colors against a background of greenery and brown treetrunks. Flowers, hats, basket, and parasol form a series of bright areas that only enhance the black dress in the center. Here we should note the superb piece of painting that well deserves separate enlargement — the white parasol and blue-ribboned hat tossed carelessly upon the grass in the left-hand corner, as if they had some symbolic significance, perhaps representing the artist's signature.

In the pastel *On the Lawn,* *** we find the same children and the same young woman, but this time she is seated in the longer summer grass, with a child on her lap, forming a rigid, almost hieratic pyramid that contrasts with the movement of the landscape, where the bent branches, tall central tree, and half-hidden flowerbed on the right give the picture a life of its own. Very different is the movement in *Catching Butterflies.* **** We still see the same garden, but the young woman stands in the center, in a white dress obliquely crossed by the handle of the butterfly net, her pose parallel with the bare trunk of the small tree beside her, and seems with her sad eyes to make time stand still. Here it is the play of light, falling through the branches and lying in pools on the ground, that gives the picture its vitality.

Nevertheless, beyond the sparkling gaiety of the light we can often glimpse in Morisot's pictures a sad gaze, a child huddled in a corner, or a pose that seems tinged with melancholy, and it is this juxtaposition of apparent happiness and hidden sadness that is the secret of Berthe Morisot's work; as if she had transposed, in a universe where all seems harmony, Baudelaire's definition of beauty as not existing unless enhanced by some slight

---

* See page 22.   ** See page 26.   *** See page 27.   **** See page 23.

Nude Seen in Back View, 1889. Drypoint, 5¹⁄₈″ × 3⁵⁄₈″ (13 × 9.2 cm)
Bibliothèque Nationale, Paris

defect. A woman of deep feelings, all her life she was restless and often sad, as we can infer from a few brief words in a letter or notebook, and it is this that explains the haunting looks and gestures that sometimes appear in her pictures.

Another beautiful, typically Impressionist landscape of the same period is *In the Cornfield* (1875, Louvre Museum). It is all horizontal lines, except for a young boy in the foreground, emerging from the corn as if from the sea, the only blue touch among so much yellow and green. Edouard Manet admired the picture, which was painted at Genevilliers, and it was one of the things that inspired him after he had changed his mind about the new Impressionist painting and, on Berthe Morisot's advice, decided to paint in the open air.

At one of the Impressionist exhibitions, Berthe Morisot's former teacher, Guichard, was horrified to find his pupil in such company and wrote to her mother: « It is not safe to live with madmen ... they are all a bit touched. » In spite of his exaggerated fears, he was nevertheless absolutely right when he accused her of « having wanted to do in oils what is exclusively the province of watercolor, » adding: « to be the best watercolorist of one's time is a fate that is enviable enough. »

*
*   *

The second half of the nineteenth century is one of the great periods in the history of watercolors. As a technique it was admirably suited to the spirit of the time, with its rapid application and ability to capture the passing moment or render in a few allusive touches the most transient scenes or landscapes. It was not long before watercolors became a symbol of Impressionism.

Berthe Morisot was indeed one of the greatest watercolor painters. Some of her biographers say that she did not really start painting in watercolors until the siege of Paris (September 1870 – January 1871) when she was unable to go beyond her own garden to look for subjects to paint. In fact, she began in 1864 with *Girl on a Bench*, which is influenced by Corot, and *Rosalie Riesener* (Louvre Museum) in 1866, which breathes the spirit of Delacroix and Gavarni; but it is true that *On the Sofa** is dated 1871. Here the colors are so fresh they might have been applied only a moment ago, the red of the armchair contrasting with the blue of the skirt, the whole made more vivid by the slight Tachism that outlines the profile. And in the same year she produced the *Woman and Child Seated in a Meadow*, which was afterward acquired by Degas and proved to be one of her most successful and fertile themes.

In 1872 she painted *On the Balcony*** a sketch for the oil painting of the same name, as well as *Woman and Child on a Bench* (Louvre Museum) where, against a delicate woodland background, a young woman is sitting in a faintly patterned dress, the only distinctive detail being the black-edged collar (although still without the famous ribbons that would soon be Morisot's signature).

Next she painted a major series of watercolors in rapid succession. *On the Cliff* (1873, Louvre Museum) shows a young woman seated in profile shading her face from the sun, and merging with the background so that she seems almost to become part of the landscape. *Woman and Child by the Sea**** was painted in 1874 and later belonged in turn

---

* See page 19. ** See page 20. *** See page 28.

YOUNG WOMAN AND CHILD SITTING IN THE GRASS, 1875. Pastel, 6¼″ × 8⅝″ (16 × 22 cm)
Private Collection, Paris

Julie in the Apple-Tree, 1889. Red chalk, 9½" × 14⅜" (24 × 36.5 cm)
Private Collection, Paris

to the collectors Henri Rouart, Jacques Doucet, and David-Weill. In this picture, with a few brief touches the painter captures both time and space, the fleeting moment but also the impression of permanence.

This was followed by a lovely, transparent *Genevilliers*, and afterward the *Young Woman and Child Sitting in the Grass.** It was painted in the same year (1875) near Cambrai whose windmills can be seen faintly outlined against the sky.

As we have seen, same of these watercolors are studies for pictures, but others are works in their own right and it is possible to follow the progress of an art that was becoming increasingly allusive over the years. Two of the most succesful examples are the *Lady out Walking* of 1883, an abstract before its time, and the *Lady with a Parasol Sitting in a Park.***

During the summer of 1875, the first year of her marriage, Berthe Morisot went to England by way of the Isle of Wight, where she painted a memorable oil, *Eugène Manet in the Isle of Wight.**** Seated on the extreme left, Eugène Manet is looking out of an open

---

* See page 49.   ** See page 68.   *** See back cover.

window over a small garden to the harbor and the ladies passing by. It is a simple, everyday scene, but the long rectangle formed between the top of the garden fence and the bottom of the open sash window, with its glimpse of boats and a little girl and a woman with her face concealed by the window frame, appears to be seen through the eyes of Eugène Manet, or as if it were the aperture of a camera which, by focusing on both dream and reality, looks forward to the technique of the cinema. Here Berthe Morisot is no less daring and original than Degas himself.

Soon too she would rival Monet in her painting of *Summer's Day*,* with two young women in a boat, the one seen full face and the other in profile, and of which we know both the finished version and the watercolor sketch. It was the first of a series of pictures inspired by the Bois de Boulogne with its ladies out walking, pale swans, and reflections in the water.

Morisot probably used the same two models for the *Women Picking Flowers* of the same year (Stockholm Museum). There is a similar contrast between blue and white, the hats are an identical straw color and there is the same blue and green background, but the horizon that ends at the level of the water in the first picture is here brought higher by the trees. And yet when placed side by side, the two paintings might almost be stills from a film.

What seems surprising today is that Morisot's pictures have been overlooked or dismissed as minor examples of Impressionism when in reality they break new ground. *Summer's Day*, for example, was shown at the Impressionist Exhibition of 1880, eight years before Monet's painting on the same subject.

It is interesting that in these open air scenes, the faces are no more than suggested, as if the features were absorbed by the light, so that they no longer have any outlines but are only pale patches of color reflecting the light in the same way as the clothes or the grass. It is all part of the influence of watercolors on oil painting. The subject is no longer rendered with the help of memory but directly through the sensation it produces, until it becomes the projection of a single moment, inseparable from the atmosphere in which it occurs. Hence the impression of lightness, transparency, and spontaneity.

Sometimes, however, in the eighties — one of the most original periods in her work — Morisot would paint a face that is clearly outlined, as if gently modeled by the light. One example is *Young Girl by the Window*,** a painting that may well have inspired Manet when he was painting his last pictures at Bellevue or Reuil, not only because of its quick brushstrokes but also by the way in which the light is suggested and caught in the gleaming texture of the roses.

Another sensitive and strikingly intense portrait is the one she painted of her nephew Marcel Gobillard — *Little Boy in Gray*.*** The quick, light brushstrokes and background of bold flowers only render more lifelike the child painted in close-up with his boater in his hand, in an attitude that is determined but by no means stilted or stiff.

An interesting example of the diversity of Berthe Morisot's work is provided by the *Lady at her Toilette*,**** where the subject seems to dissolve in a cloud of powder and dazzling light. Here Berthe Morisot appears once again to have been ahead of her Impressionist friends, for the picture shows a freedom of style that would not be carried so far until Monet painted his *Water Lilies*.

Unfortunately, it was a freedom that was not appreciated by those who should have been the most enlightened critics of the day. One example is J. K. Huysmans, with his unusual

---

* See page 41.　　** See page 73.　　*** See page 30.　　**** See page 35.

GARDEN AT BOUGIVAL, 1884
Oil on canvas, 28³/₈″ × 36¹/₄″ (72 × 92 cm)
Private Collection

Little Saint John, 1890
Pencil, 14¹/₈″ × 22⁷/₈″ (36 × 58 cm) ▷
Private Collection, Paris

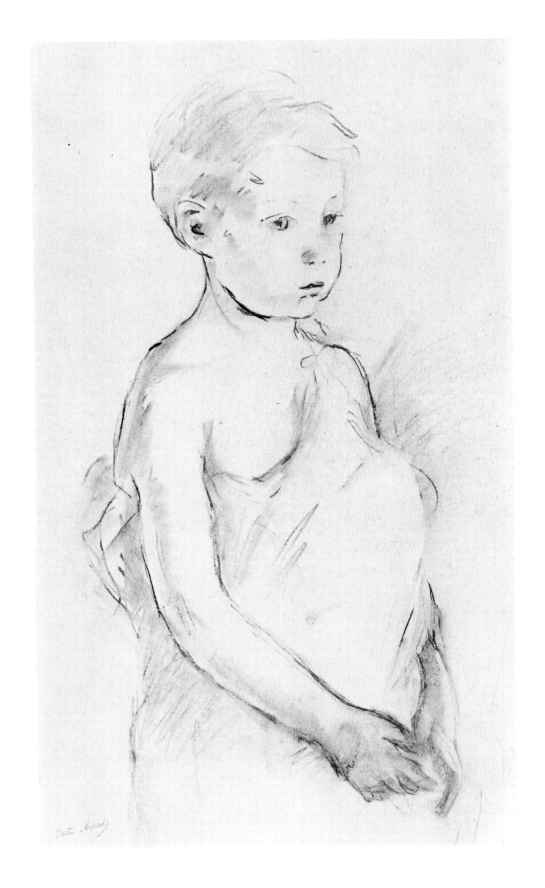

Standing Bather, 1888
Red chalk
18½" × 11¾"
(47 × 30 cm)
Private Collection

views and sharp tongue, at once curious and reticent, who confessed to being attracted but not won over by Berthe Morisot. He preferred Mary Cassat whose paintings seemed to him «more harmonious, more peaceful, more learned.» He blamed Berthe Morisot for leaving her work «at the sketching stage ... (nothing but) a bright pink and white fog,» adding something which, with the benefit of hindsight, may well make us smile today: «It is magnetized Chaplin,* with the addition of a turbulence of agitated and tense nerves.» The description would seem to apply more to Huysmans than to Morisot. And he goes on to say: «An exhilarating fashionable elegance emanates from her morbid sketches, those surprising improvisations to which the epithet hysterical might well be applied.» The combination of exhilarating and morbid, improvisation and hysteria might have come straight out of «A Rebours» («Against Nature»), which was, in fact, published in 1887. It is difficult for an critic, if he looks no further than the surface, to avoid projecting his own personality on to what he sees and assimilating the painter's world with his own fantasies, convinced of being an impartial spectator when he is only making a subjective and probably erroneous interpretation. In any case, it is interesting to note how Huysmans was neither quite right nor entirely wrong in his judgments, it is just that everything is distorted by the choice of words. Not only does his mistrust of women make it hard for him to succumb to her charm, but his attitude reveals the enormous gulf which separates Impressionism from Naturalism.

Berthe Morisot found another original subject in the skaters on the frozen lake in the Bois de Boulogne. It was something that should have interested Huysmans and that had not been done since the Dutch painters of the the seventeenth century — and then only in the form of crowd scenes. It is true that Manet painted his *Skating* in 1877, but that was a fashionable picture, an excuse for showing the analogy between the skates biting into the ice and the torsades on the dress of the figure in the foreground. What the «beautiful painter,» as a friend of her mother had once described Berthe Morisot, chose to paint was a *Young Woman Retying her Skate.*** The picture is a symphony of three colors: a blue that is almost black (the young woman), a white touched sometimes with blue and sometimes with pink, and the deep pink of the winter sky with the trees outlined agains it. Yet again everything is suggested, allusive, hinted at, painted in the lightes of strokes applied with the tip of the brush. We are reminded of the subtlety of Mallarmé and his words that are so close to music. The picture shows not only the influence of watercolors but also the contribution of pastels to Berthe Morisot's delicate and accurate palette.

*
*   *

A few years earlier, in April 1877, one of her first admirers, Philippe Burty, noted:

> She uses pastels with the freedom and charm of Rosalba Carriera in the eighteenth century ... she is a delicate colorist who paints everything in a general harmony of white, which is difficult to achieve without lapsing into affectation.

---

* Charles Chaplin (1825–1891), French painter, quite well-known in his days. ** See page 44.

The Aloes of Cimiez, 1889
◁ *Lead pencil, 8⅞″ × 11⅜″ (23 × 29 cm)*
Private Collection, Paris

WOMAN AND CHILD IN A GARDEN, 1884
Oil on canvas, 23¼″ × 28⅜″ (59 × 72 cm)
National Gallery of Scotland, Edinburgh

Not until 1871 did Berthe Morisot begin to use pastels consistently — the catalogue of her works mentions only two before that date — but from then on the technique became one of her favorite methods of working. In *Portrait of Madame Pontillon** the composition remains classical but the mellow treatment of the great black garment contrasts with the hastily drawn patterns on the curtains or the puckered appearance of the sofa. The duality is repeated in the two halves of the face, almost as if she was painting her sister on the right and herself on the left. Or perhaph unconsciously Berthe Morisot had portrayed the two sides of her own nature, a dichotomy that pervaded her life and was trascended in her work.

Fécamp and Maurecourt provided subjects for pastels. *On the Beach* (1874) is an expanded version of the watercolor *Woman and Child by the Sea*, while the pastel *On the Lawn* is an exercise in the contrast between stillness and movement. As we saw in discussing the *Young Woman Retying her Skate*, Morisot's mastery of pastels enriched her painting, and the interplay of the three techniques — watercolors, pastels, and oils — would provide enough material for a whole series of research on the differences and similarities, and the discoveries, inventions, and innovations involved. Only Degas was doing anything as complex at the time. And Morisot is certainly his equal in her pastel picture of her niece *Paule Gobillard,*** sitting drawing. The composition is admirably severe and rigorous, with the soft blue crossed by bars of dark brown, the classical statue on a pillar and the studious model bending over her drawing board, the long plait continuing the line of her profile.

*
*   *

Berthe Morisot's work contains a number of themes that perhaps appear too earnest for modern taste, but the style in which they are treated is anything but labored. One example is the *Woman Sitting Sewing*, in the Pau Museum. The light transfigures her face and caresses her shoulders, while the garden full of roses gives the picture a festive air. Another is the *Fable,*** where a young woman on a bench talks to the child in front of her, and the two figures seem to be bathed in light, so that the colors unfold like the petals of a flower. Here we should recall something that can never be said too often: in art, the subject matters little, it is how it is treated that is important; in this case, the way in which the ordinary everyday scene is transformed into something that is truer than reality, for all the hidden dimensions are revealed by the artist in the play of colors and brushwork, while imperceptible echoes are made clear in the sparkle and gleam of light.

One of the major contributions of Impressionism — but also of any artistic movement that has sought new techniques in order to capture reality on canvas — is to have conveyed everyday life, in scenes never thought of before, and to have made the humdrum a base for marvelous feats of invention where nothing is taken for granted and all must be rediscovered. If Impressionism is still capable both of attracting crowds and inspiring artists, it is because it succeds in suggesting reality by reducing it to a series of luminous dots that somehow render the world more accurately than the most painstakingly detailed imitation.

Now that Berthe Morisot had «entered the positive stage of life» as she wrote to her brother soon after her marriage, the birth of her daughter provided her with endless

---

* See page 17.   ** See page 31.   *** See page 39.

opportunities for finding magic in everyday life. Julie, with her constant presence, her playfulness, her smile, and gestures, was her mother's favorite model for fifteen years, very often in the company of her cousins or friends. Berthe painted her most frequently at their holiday home at Bougival, where they spent four successive summers from 1881 onward, in a house surrounded by a garden full of trees and flowers: roses and clematis, irises and peonies.

There Morisot painted some of her few pictures of men — not counting the portrait of the *Little Boy in Gray*, the drawings for the *Little Saint John*,* and the *Picnic.* One of these pictures shows her husband, Eugène Manet, sitting on a camp stool reading, with his daughter opposite him. Here the brushstrokes defining trees, grass, and figures are applied in opposing directions so that they create a kind of circular movement. Two years later in another version of *Eugène Manet and his Daughter in the Garden,*** the figures are shown in close up and the composition is enlivened by a play of oblique lines and by the contrast between the greens and the browns of the garden and the light colors of the flowers and the child's dress.

---

* See page 53.   ** See page 43.

Nude Shepherdess Lying down, 1891. Red chalk, 14⅝" × 21¼" (37 × 54 cm)
Private Collection

IN THE DINING ROOM, 1886. Oil on canvas, $23^5/_8'' \times 19^5/_{16}''$ (60 × 49 cm)
National Gallery of Art, Washington, D.C. Ailsa Mellon Bruce Collection

Berthe Morisot with Daughter Julie, 1887. Lead pencil, 10¼″ × 7½″ (26 × 19 cm)
Private Collection

The high point of Morisot's painting at that house was undoubtedly *Garden at Bougival*,* one of her most subtle and almost abstract works. A glimpse of the sky, a few square roofs on the left, and one or two roses in the center are the only recognizable things in the picture. All the rest is efflorescence, exuberance, rapid, dynamic brushstrokes — in other words, pure painting. The picture was painted at a time when the Impressionist group was beginning to split up, and when two painters would be responsible for carrying the movement to extremes: one was Berthe Morisot who only had ten more years to live and the other was Claude Monet who went on working until the first quarter of the twentieth century.

The same exuberance is to be found in *The Doll on the Veranda*,** but here there are a number of clearly identifiable objects: the houses opposite, the foreground with a table and teapot, and a chair with a doll sitting in it, as well as the wooden post that divides the landscape vertically into two unequal halves.

This picture must be looked at in conjunction with another larger painting entitled *On the Veranda*,*** where objects like the venetian blind and the windowpane, which were no more than suggested in the first version, are now clearly visible, while the diffuse light of the first canvas is here reflected from two sources: the carafe in the foreground and the litlle girl's hair.

The central tree in *Woman and Child in a Garden*,**** also painted at Bougival, seems to be the pivot around which the grass is spinning, so that the rapid style that seeks to capture the impression before it disappears or the light changes is here accompanied by the sensation of a wild dance of nature, slowed only by the human figures.

From Bougival, Berthe Morisot sometimes crossed the Seine in the direction of Pontoise and paid a visit to Maurecourt, where in 1884 she painted a picture with the same title as one dated ten years earlier: *In the Garden at Maurecourt*.***** There are several watercolor sketches for the later picture, as well as a number of alternative versions in oils. The style is much more free and daring than in the earlier painting. The sky is no longer visible, as if the painter had spread out her canvas on the ground, the trees are no longer defined by lines but by strokes, and the grass is crushed beneath the paintbrush as if someone had lain on it, while the silhouette of the back of the little girl in the foreground has become almost transparent.

Throughout her life Berthe Morisot returned to the same subjects, evoking a familiar atmosphere but always with a new and enriched composition. For example, the *Cottage Interior******* painted in Jersey in 1886, is reminiscent of *Eugene Manet in the Isle of Wight*, with its single figure near a window opening on to a seaside landscape. But this time the child in her beautiful luminous dress seems to take no interest in the view but to be no more than the central figure of this scene in which the subject matter is of far less importance than the painting. Surely the treatment of the table anticipates Bonnard: cloth, cup and fruit are all exercises in pure painting. But we cannot help noting certain analogies that may have escaped the painter, for example, the napkin in the foreground folded like a swan that seems to float on a watery mirror.

*

*   *

---

* See page 52.   ** See page 81.   *** See page 42.   **** See page 57.   ***** See page 66.
****** See page 65.

Embroidering, 1889. Lead pencil, $7\frac{1}{2}'' \times 8\frac{5}{8}''$ (19 × 22 cm)
Musée du Petit Palais, Paris

Rather too much emphasis has been laid on the influence of Renoir on the second part of Berthe Morisot's work. Clearly the two painters share a common inspiration and there are similarities between some of their paintings — not always the most successful ones. They saw each other frequently and sometimes worked on the same subjects, but all the Impressionists did this in their constant search for less cumbersome and more subtle ways of grasping reality. As we shall see, at the end of the 1880s Berthe Morisot went back to drawing to give her pictures a more obvious structure, while at the same time retaining the vivacity and lightness of touch so characteristic of her style.

Pastels like *The Piano*,* or *Young Girl with a Basket*,** as well as pictures painted in rapid succession like *The Cherry Tree*,*** *Young Girls at the Window*,**** and *Beneath the Orange Tree*,***** undoubtedly have something in common with a number of Renoir's paintings. There are the same twisted trees, the same fondness for hair tied back underneath a hat, and the same scattering of gleams of light. However, if we look more closely at *The Cherry Tree*, for example, which exists in three versions, not to mention a number of drawings and watercolors, we can see that the hidden strength of the picture stems from the juxtaposition of two complementary rhythms. On the one hand there is the upward movement of the girl standing on tiptoe to hold up her basket, and prolonged by the ladder behind her; and on the other hand the downward flow of the fruit-laden branches and the bright dress of the girl standing on the ladder and picking cherries. The dynamics of the composition are very different from that of Renoir who either more sensuously conceals form beneath color, preferring more horizontal rhythms, or else, still toward the end of the 1880s, attempts to make the Impressionist style much more smooth and rounded (*The Dance*, *The Bathers*), moving away from the values of Impressionism toward a classicism inspired by Italy. Berthe Morisot was never tempted to retrace her steps in this way.

Of course, there are analogies between the two painters, and resemblances that are obvious if only skin-deep, but to seek, out of mental laziness, to make them extend to Berthe Morisot's entire later work is to be bigoted, blind, or deliberately misleading. The fact is that parallel with the paintings which resemble Renoir and which were perhaps only an unfinished experiment interrupted by her death, throughout her last years Berthe Morisot was also producing works that have little connection with Renoir at all. And here we must speak not so much of influence but of convergence, a subtle form of transposition, closer to the work of a poet: we are thinking of Stéphane Mallarmé.

*
*   *

Berthe Morisot seems to echo all that is most sensitive and feminine in Mallarmé. She of all painters is most like the poet. Her pictures resemble the quatrains he used to write on his envelopes, full of flowing allusions and subtle delicacy of feeling. The paintings are not, of course, as esoteric as Mallarmé's language, but both reach the essential in the same way, with the same light touch, the same skimming over the surface of reality. Berthe Morisot also chooses similar subjects, like the series of landscapes and swans in the Bois de Boulogne in which a whole scene is miraculously conjured up with the merest hint of color and a few deft strokes of the brush.

---

* See page 89.   ** See page 74.   *** See page 82.   **** See page 88.   ***** See page 86.

COTTAGE INTERIOR (or GIRL WITH A DOLL), 1886. Oil on canvas, $19\frac{5}{8}'' \times 23\frac{5}{8}''$ (50 × 60 cm)
Musée d'Ixelles, Brussels

IN THE GARDEN AT MAURECOURT, 1884. Oil on canvas, 21¼″ × 25⅝″ (54 × 65 cm)
The Toledo Museum of Art, Ohio. Gift of Edward Drummond Libbey

Landscape (Jersey), 1886. Watercolor, $9^{13}/_{16}''\times 12^5/_8''$ (25 × 32 cm)
Ashmoleum Museum, Oxford

Lady with a Parasol Sitting in a Park, 1885
Watercolor on paper, $7^1/_2''$ × $8^3/_{16}''$ (19 × 20.8 cm)
The Metropolitan Museum of Art, New York. Harris Brisbane Dick Fund

The Lake at Bois de Boulogne, 1888
Drypoint, 6⅛" × 4½" (15.5 × 11.5 cm)
Bibliothèque Nationale, Paris

The Goose, 1889
Drypoint, 5⅝″ × 4½″ (14.2 × 11.3 cm)
Bibliothèque Nationale, Paris

The Duck, 1888
Drypoint, 5³|₈″ × 3¹⁵|₁₆″ (13.7 × 10 cm)
Bibliothèque Nationale, Paris

It is in this set of works, which come very close to abstraction, that we can see what is perhaps Berthe Morisot's most original attribute, that feeling for transparency that was never as highly developed by any of the other Impressionists. Pictures like *Swans on the Lake*, which belonged to Paul Valéry, or *Swans in Autumn*, reach the ineffable through this sense of transparency, which, far more than a new technique, is, in fact, an attempt to grasp what lies behind appearances. Other examples are an engraving like *The Goose** or a painting like *Julie Manet and her Greyhound Laertes*** — Laertes was a present from Mallarmé to Berthe Morisot. Here the chair and the dress are not completely painted in so that the undercoat shows through and gives an impression of shimmering, vibrant light.

Mallarmé and Berthe Morisot had been friends for a great many years, and when she died the poet became Julie Manet's guardian for the few remaining years of his life.

In 1887 or 1888 Stéphane Mallarmé asked Berthe Morisot, Degas, and Renoir if they would illustrate one of his future collections: «The Lacquer Mirror.» Morisot had done very little engraving but she set to work and produced a number of plates, at least two of which appear to be related to Mallarmé's project: *The Lake at Bois de Boulogne* and *The Duck****. The book did not come out with that title or in that particular form and Morisot's plates were long unpublished. And yet it is hard to imagine anything more fluid and more in keeping with the spirit of Mallarmé than these etchings where nothing is overemphasized but everything is expressed with an exquisite sense of light, in a style that is stripped to essentials.

Before that Berthe Morisot had made engravings of some of her own pictures or drawings, for example, her *Self-Portrait with her Daughter Julie,**** a *Nude Seen in Back View,***** a *Young Woman Resting,****** or *Julie Manet with a Cat*, which was inspired by a picture by Renoir. But that was the end of her career as an engraver.

At about the same time she began to take a new interest in drawing. Almost all the drawings can be dated with certainty as they are preliminary sketches for pictures and nearly all of them were done at the end of the 1880s or in the early 1890s.

*
*   *

Nevertheless, although briefly it looked as if Berthe Morisot were seeking to achieve a more solid structure, it can never be sufficiently stressed that during those last years she was simultaneously carrying out a very different form of research that would lead her to reduce everything to flecks of color or indications of light. Unfortunately, she did not have time to bring to perfection the techniques that afterward Bonnard succeeded in applying. What is striking about all her last works is less the impression that they are unfinished, which is only true of the very last pictures, than a feeling of progress brutally interrupted: it was as though everything that she glimpsed, discovered, and captured for a moment during those final years was no sooner conquered than lost again, as if dashed from her grasp by death.

---

    * See page 70.   ** See page 84.   *** See pages 69 and 71.   **** See page 61 (the drawing from which she made the engraving).   ***** See page 47.   ****** See page 79.

YOUNG GIRL BY THE WINDOW, 1878. Oil on canvas, 29¹⁵/₁₆″ × 24″ (76 × 61 cm)
Musée Fabre, Montpellier, France

YOUNG GIRL WITH A BASKET, 1891
Pastel, 22¹/₁₆″ × 15³/₈″ (56 × 39 cm)
Musée Marmottan, Paris

MADEMOISELLE LOUISE RIESENER, 1888
Charcoal and pastel on paper, 22¹/₁₆″ × 18¹/₂″ (56 × 47 cm)
The Cleveland Museum of Art. Leonard C. Hanna, Jr. Bequest

YOUNG GIRL WITH A CAT, 1892. Oil `on canvas, 21⅝″ × 18″ (55 × 46 cm)
Private Collection

2 mars 93

Julie Manet, 1893. Pencil, 8⁷/₈″ × 13³/₄″ (22.5 × 35 cm)
Private Collection, Paris

One of the most successful paintings of those years is the *Model Resting** of 1887, where objects are suggested entirely by the way they reflect the light. Between a mirror, a screen, and a chair, a young woman in the nude half covers her body with a blue peignoir which she holds with her arms folded against her breast. This is the beginning of a series of paintings of women in which sensuality is so intimately incorporated with the style that the brush itself becomes a caress. Here, and in the *Self-Portrait*** painted in 1885 on an unprepared canvas, we are reminded for a moment of an earlier version of Lautrec. The paint is spread thinly over the canvas in a series of rapid strokes, but this Lautrec is more gentle than caustic, more sensual than licentious. Nor should we forget, in noting the technical similarity between the two painters, that Lautrec had not yet painted any of his major works. What is curious about these paintings by Morisot, or at least it must have seemed odd to the people who saw them for the first time, is that the lighter the touch, the stronger is the power of suggestion.

Perhaps the most moving thing about her last pictures is that life is so subtly captured in the rendering of sensuality and yet at the same time it seems to be slipping away like water through the fingers of a hand. Examples of the new sense of voluptuousness are to be found in the supple lines of the *Nude Shepherdess Lying Down,**** a red chalk drawing done at Mézy in 1891, as well as the various pictures for which Jeanne Fourmanoir was a model. We can recognize her features in *On the Lake* (1892), where she is seated in a boat, with the neck of the swan echoing the rhythm of her dress, and in the *Cherry Tree* painted in the garden at Mézy in 1891. Above all she is to be seen in the two most beautiful paintings of 1892, works which in some ways may be considered as the culmination of Berthe Morisot's art. One is the *Sleeping Girl* which brings to mind a line by Valéry:

Sleeping girl, golden mass of shadows and abandonment,

and the other the *Young Girl with a Cat,***** all in shades of gold and green: two aspects of a sensuality that is allusive and discrete and yet suggestive of fulfillment and secret fire.

With its few swans half hidden by the mist, the *Forest Interior in Autumn,***** painted during the last months of 1894, seems like a farewell to life. The minute, scarcely identifiable figures almost disappear beneath the mass of color. They carry no more weight than all the other areas of paint in this picture where color is so much more important than form. Between the green of the tree trunks and the pink of the carpet of leaves, a touch of blue in the center represents the horizon or hints at another world.

At the beginning of 1895 Berthe Morisot fell ill while looking after her daughter. By the beginning of March she was dead. Only a few months before, at Rue Weber, she had painted *Julie Daydreaming*******. And just before her death, the last words she wrote were addressed to her daughter:

My little Julie, I love you on my deathbed; I shall go on loving you after I am dead; please don't cry for me; the separation was inevitable...

---

* See page 85.   ** See title page.   *** See page 59.   **** See page 76.   ***** See page 83.
****** See page 91.

Young Woman Resting, 1889. Drypoint, 2¹⁵/₁₆″ × 4¹/₂″ (7.5 × 11.3 cm)
Private Collection, Paris

Berthe Morisot died at the age of fifty-four after a quiet life in which intensity of feeling was masked by her natural reticence but sometimes revealed in her work. Perhaps her final message is to be found in a hastily scribbled notebook where she confirms what is hinted at in a number of her portraits, in a mixture of doubt, renunciation, lucidity, passion, and understatement:

> With what resignation one reaches the end of life, resigned to all the failures of this life and all the uncertainties of the next one, it is a long time since I have hoped for anything and the desire for glorification after death seems to me an excessive ambition; mine would be confined to seeking to capture something of the passing moment, oh, only something! The least little thing! and yet even that ambition is excessive.

This unassuming, disillusioned testimony throws light on the depth of Morisot's feelings, the constantly flickering flame threatened always by unfathomable sadness ... What she did not know, however, in writing those lines was that her work would transcend all her doubts and begin the long, sometimes subterranean journey toward the future.

Berthe Morisot's work comprise 416 oil paintings, 191 pastels, 240 watercolors, 8 engravings, 2 sculptures, and 200 or 300 hundred drawings. It is slightly less than Manet's output, and a great deal less than the production of Monet, Degas, or Renoir. But we should not forget that Berthe Morisot died at the age of fifty-four, the first among the artists of the Impressionist group.

*
*　　*

In concluding this brief account, it is time to dispel one of the most persistent misunderstandings about Morisot's work: the famous feminine charm with which she is credited but which immediately makes her suspect as an artist. The fact that her work is full of charm is undeniable, but at the same time her art goes far deeper than the worn-out, hackneyed phrases that have been used to describe it for more than a century. We at least have the benefit of hindsight and it is up to us to place her achievements in their true perspective.

A woman who painted other women, Berthe Morisot endowed her models with all the charm, sensuality, and tenderness of her own vision of womanhood. Yet at the same time her paintings are in no way inferior to those of the greatest and most creative artists of her time—Manet, Monet, Degas, and Renoir. As we have already seen, she was their equal when it came to quality, inventiveness, and strength. Moreover, in comparison with the other two women artists of her own day or shortly afterward—Mary Cassatt and Suzanne Valadon—she has the advantage of never having fallen into the trap of excessive muscularity or falsely masculine toughness.

It is for us to see that beyond the delicate, feminine touch, Morisot's art is well structured and constantly in search of more subtle means of expression, while at the same time the very felicity of the style both conceals and reveals depths that only the artist's deliberate understatement has masked from too hasty eyes.

*
*　　*

When themes have been too often painted, their impact can only be restored by a new or long-forgotten approach. In the same way, if we get too close to reality, we must blur the edges and reduce the content and, if we would get closer still, even dissolve the image itself. Then forms are replaced by light; dense, clearly defined volumes give way to areas of color, and explicit symbols are replaced by ellipsis or allusion.

Introduced to painting by Corot, and working parallel with Manet, who preached realism but transfigured it by his powers of invention and his smooth and rapid technique, Berthe Morisot brought to the vision of reality not only the full range of sensuality and feminine charm but also the unusual strength she derived from a mixture of sadness and

THE DOLL ON THE VERANDA, 1884. Oil on canvas, 19⅝″ × 18⅞″ (50 × 48 cm)
Private Collection

FOREST INTERIOR IN AUTUMN
1894
Oil on canvas
$16^{15}/_{16}'' \times 13''$ (43 × 33 cm)
Private Collection
▷

◁
THE CHERRY TREE, 1891
Oil on canvas, $60^5/_8'' \times 31^1/_2''$
(154 × 80 cm)
Private Collection

Julie Manet and
her Greyhound Laerte, 1893
Oil on canvas
28³/₄″ × 31¹/₂″ (73 × 80 cm)
Musée Marmottan, Paris

Model Resting, 1887
Oil on canvas
25⁵/₈″ × 21¹/₄″ (65 × 54 cm) ▷
Private Collection

BENEATH THE ORANGE TREE, 1889. Oil on canvas, 21¼″ × 25⅝″ (54 × 65 cm)
Private Collection

Study for « The Mozart Sonata », 1894.   Pencil, 8⅝" × 11¾" (22 × 30 cm)
Private Collection, Paris

YOUNG GIRLS AT THE WINDOW, 1892
Oil on canvas
◁ 25⁵/₈″ × 19⁵/₁₆″ (65 × 49 cm)
Private Collection, Paris

THE PIANO, 1888
Pastel, 25⁵/₈″ × 31⁷/₈″ (65 × 81 cm)
Private Collection, Paris

lucidity. Gradually she plunged deeper into the heart of reality, capturing the light in bright flashes and, without entirely dissolving the image, increasingly investing it with the kind of luminosity whose source is nowhere visible but whose presence is all-pervading.

Her research on light led her to consider returing to more definite outlines and more substantial forms, but her last pictures indicate that the quest was by no means finished when death took her. This woman who seemed all her life to have painted for her own pleasure, as if art were no more than a pleasant distraction, had in fact pursued with passion, tenacity, and clear-sightedness an adventure where ease was only a mask and charm concealed rigor and strength, so that when she appeared to have done no more than brush the surface of the canvas, she had nevertheless gone beyond and dissolved appearances and miraculously enriched our vision.

JEAN DOMINIQUE REY

JULIE DAYDREAMING, 1894. Oil on canvas, 25¼″ × 21¼″ (64 × 54 cm)
Private Collection, Paris

BIOGRAPHY

1841   Berthe Morisot was born on January 15 at Bourges where her father, Tiburce Morisot, was prefect. She was the third of four children.

1848   Brief stay at Limoges where her father was again prefect.

1855   After Tiburce Morisot's resignation, the family moved to Rue des Moulins (now Rue Scheffer) in Paris. Berthe Morisot had piano lessons with Stamaty.

1857   The three sisters, Yves, Edma, and Berthe, had their first drawing lessons with Chocarne, but Edma and Berthe were disappointed and continued their studies with Guichard who lived in the same street as they did.

1860–1862   Guichard, foreseeing the gifts of the two sisters, told them: « What you need now is Corot. » The two girls joined the studio of the famous artist who dined with the Morisots every Tuesday.

1863   Corot recommended Edma and Berthe to his pupil Oudinot who lived near Auvers, where they met Daubigny, Daumier and Guillemet.

1864   The two sisters exhibited for the first time at the Salon. The Morisots spent the summer in the house of the painter Riesener at Beuzeval.

1866   Visit to Brittany and pictures painted at Pont-Aven.

1868   Berthe Morisot met Manet in the Louvre. She posed for *The Balcony*. She met Degas with the Manets.

1869   Her sister Edma gave up painting on her marriage. Berthe stayed with her at Lorient and painted a number of portraits of her and her mother.

1872   Visit to Spain and Madrid.

1874   Death of her father. First Impressionist exhibition at Nadar's. Berthe Morisot exhibited four oil paintings, two pastels, and three watercolors. In December she married Eugène Manet, the painter's brother.

1875   Visit to Genevilliers and afterward to England and the Isle of Wight where she painted several pictures.

1876   Second Impressionist exhibition. Berthe Morisot took part in all the Impressionist exhibitions except for the fourth in 1879, after the birth of her daughter Julie.

1881   Visits to Bougival and Nice where she painted a large number of pictures, and afterward Italy.

1883   Death of Edouard Manet. Berthe and her husband moved to Rue de Villejust. Impressionist exhibition at London.

1884   Last stay at Bougival.

1885   Year of intense work. Journey to Belgium and Holland.

1886   Berthe Morisot lived and worked on the Island of Jersey.

1888   Stay at Cimiez in the south of France.

1890   Moved with her husband to Mézy, to a house overlooking the Seine.

1891   From Mézy where she painted *The Cherry Tree*, Berthe Morisot and her husband discovered Le Mesnil, which they bought and where she retired for a time on the death of her husband.

1892   In May, first solo exhibition at Boussod and Valadon.

1893   Berthe Morisot moved to Rue Weber. Her daughter Julie, Jeanne Fourmanoir, and Lucie Léon sat for her as models. Stay at Fontainebleau where she was Mallarmé's neighbor.

1894   Exhibited at the Libre Esthétique in Brussels. On the instigation of Mallarmé, the State bought her *Girl Dressed for the Ball*. Visit to Brittany.

1895   After a short illness, Berthe Morisot died on March 2.

BIBLIOGRAPHY

All the main works on Impressionism give considerable space to Berthe Morisot, in particular:

DURET, Th. *Les Peintres impressionistes*. Paris, 1878 and 1906.

FÉNÉON, F. *Les Impressionnistes en 1886*. Paris, 1886.

MAUCLAIR, C. *L'Impressionnisme*. Paris, 1904.

REWALD, J. *The History of Impressionism*. New York, 1961.

COGNIAT, R. *The Century of the Impressionists*. New York, 1976 (rev. ed.).

MONNERET, S. *L'Impressionnisme et son époque*. Paris, 1979.

The following works contain studies on Berthe Morisot:

GEOFFROY, G. *La Vie artistique*. 3rd series. Paris, 1894; id., 6th series, Paris, 1900.

HUYSMANS, J. K. *L'Art moderne*. Paris, 1903, republished 1975.

WYZEWA, Th. de. *Peintres de jadis et d'aujourd'hui*. Paris, 1903.

MARX, R. *Maîtres d'hier et d'aujourd'hui*. Paris, 1914.

BLANCHE, J. E. *Propos de peintre*. 2nd series. Paris, 1923.

Any approach to the life and work of Berthe Morisot must begin with two essential sources:

D. ROUART, ed. *The Correspondence of Berthe Morisot*. New York, 1959.

BATAILLE, M. L. and G. WILDENSTEIN. *Catalogue raisonné of the oil paintings, pastels and watercolors of Berthe Morisot. Preface by Denis Rouart*. Paris, 1961.

Last, we should note the publication of the *Diary* of Julie Manet, Berthe Morisot's daughter (Paris: Klincksieck, 1979), containing valuable memories of the painter's last years.

Works entirely devoted to Berthe Morisot are few in number:

FOURREAU, A. *Berthe Morisot*. Paris, 1925.

ANGOULVENT, Monique. *Berthe Morisot*. Paris, 1933.

ROUART, Louis. *Berthe Morisot*. Paris, 1941.

ROUART, Denis. *Berthe Morisot*. Paris, 1949.

HUISMAN, Philippe. *Berthe Morisot*. Lausanne, 1962.

Among the notices, prefaces or articles we must at least mention:

MALLARMÉ, Stéphane. Preface to the catalogue of the 1896 exhibition, reprinted in « Divagations, » Paris, 1897.

VALÉRY, Paul. *Tante Berthe*, preface to the catalogue of the 1926 exhibition, reprinted in « Pièces sur l'Art, » Paris, 1934.

Au sujet de Berthe Morisot, preface to the catalogue of the 1941 exhibition, reprinted in « Vues, » Paris, 1948.

JAMOT, Paul. *Manet et Berthe Morisot*, Paris: « Gazette des Beaux-Arts, » January-June 1927.

ROUART, Denis. *Renoir et Berthe Morisot*, preface to the 1952 Limoges exhibition. Preface to the catalogue of the exhibition visiting Boston, New York, and San Francisco. New York 1960.

ROUART-VALÉRY, Agathe. *De « Madame Manet » à « Tante Berthe, »* « Arts, » March 1961.

SCHUHL, P. M. *L'Œuvre de Berthe Morisot, un art de vivre*, « Rivista di Estetica, » 1961.

BAILLY-HERZBERG, J. *Les estampes de Berthe Morisot*, Paris: « Gazette des Beaux-Arts, » May-June 1979.

SCOTT, William P. *The Enchanting World of Berthe Morisot*, « Art and Antiques, » 1981. The catalogue raisonné by M. L. BATAILLE contains a detailed bibliography up to 1961. An updated edition of the catalogue is in preparation.

PRINCIPAL EXHIBITIONS

Berthe Morisot took part in all the Impressionist exhibitions between 1874 and 1866, with the exception of the fourth in 1879.

1892 Paris, Boussod and Valadon (preface by G. Geoffroy). May-June.

1896 Paris, Durand - Ruel (preface by Stéphane Mallarmé). March.

1905 Paris, E. Druet. January-February.

1919 Paris, Bernheim Jeune. November.

1922 Paris, Marcel Bernheim. June-July.

1926 Paris, L. Dru (preface by Paul Valéry). May-June.

1929 Paris, Bernheim Jeune. May.

1930 London, The Leicester Galleries. March-April.

1936 New York, Wildenstein. November-December. New York, Knoedler. May-June.

1941 Paris, Orangerie Museum (preface by Paul Valery).

1948 Paris, Durand-Ruel Gallery. April.

1949 Copenhagen, Ny Carlsberg Glyptotek. August-September.

1950 London, The Arts Council.

1951 Geneva, Motte Gallery. June.

1952 Limoges, Municipal Museum. Homage to Berthe Morisot and P. A. Renoir (preface by Denis Rouart). July-October.

1952-54 Toronto, Art Gallery; New York, Metropolitan Museum; Toledo, Museum of Art; Washington, D.C., The Phillips Collection; San Francisco; Portland, Museum of Art.

1957 Dieppe, Museum. July-September.

1958 Albi, Toulouse-Lautrec Museum, July-September.

1960 New York, Wildenstein; Slatkin Galleries.

1961 London, Wildenstein.
Paris, Jacquemart-André Museum.

We wish to thank the owners of the pictures, as well as those collectors who did not want to have their names mentioned. Our special thanks to the Galerie Schmit in Paris for their valuable and kind assistance.

MUSEUMS

BELGIUM
Musée d'Ixelles, Brussels.

DENMARK
Ordrupgaardsamlingen, Copenhagen.

FRANCE
Musée Fabre, Montpellier.
Bibliothèque Nationale, Paris.
Musée du Jeu de Paume, Paris.
Musée du Louvre, Cabinet des Dessins, Paris.
Musée Marmottan, Paris.
Musée du Petit Palais, Paris.

SWEDEN
Nationalmuseum, Stockholm.

U.K.
National Gallery of Scotland, Edinburgh.
National Gallery, London.
Ashmoleum Museum, Oxford.

U.S.A.
The Art Institute of Chicago.
The Cleveland Museum of Art.
Norton Simon, Inc. Museum of Art, Los Angeles.
The Metropolitan Museum of Art, New York.
The Toledo Museum of Art, Ohio.
National Gallery of Art, Washington, D.C.

LIST OF ILLUSTRATIONS

Aloes of Cimiez (The) 56
Artist's Sister Edma with her Daughter Jeanne (The) 18
Artist's Sister, Madame Pontillon (The) 12
Artist's Sister at the Window (The) 7
At the Ball 36

Bather 45
Before the Mirror 34
Beneath the Orange Tree 86
Berthe Morisot with Daughter Julie 61
Bibi at Vassé 11

Catching Butterflies 23
Cherry-Tree (The) 82
Cottage Interior 65

Doll in the Veranda (The) 81
Duck (The) 71

Embroidering 63
Eugene Manet and his Daughter at Bougival . 38
Eugene Manet and his Daughter in the Garden 43

Fable (The) 39
Forest Interior in Autumn 83

Garden at Bougival 52
Girl in a Green Coat (Study for the) 40
Goose (The) 70

Harbor at Lorient (The) 9
Hide-and-Seek 22

In the Dining Room 60
In the Garden at Maurecourt 66
In a Villa at the Seaside 25

Julie in the Apple-Tree 50
Julie Daydreaming 91
Julie with a Mandoline 14
Julie Manet 77
Julie Manet and her Greyhound Laerte 84

Lady at her Toilette 35
Lady with a Parasol 68
Lake at Bois de Boulogne (The) 69
Landscape (Jersey) 67
Lilacs at Maurecourt (The) 26
Little Boy in Gray 30
Little Saint John 53

Mademoiselle Louise Riesener 75
Model Resting 85
Mozart Sonata (Study for the) 87

Nude seen in Back View 47
Nude Shepherdess Lying Down 59

On the Balcony 20
On the Lawn 27
On the Sofa 19
On the Veranda 42

Paule Gobillard 31
Piano (The) 89
Portrait of Madame Hubard 5
Portrait of Madame Pontillon 17

Standing Bather 54
Summer's Day 41

Thatched Cottage in Normandy 6

Woman and Child in a Garden 57
Woman and Child by the Sea 28

Young Girl with a Basket 74
Young Girl with a Cat 76
Young Girl Seated at Table 32
Young Girls at the Window 73, 88
Young Woman and Child Sitting in the Grass 49
Young Woman Powdering her Face 33
Young Woman Resting 79
Young Woman Retying her Skate 44